CHAOTIC WORLD,
quiet thoughts!

Rupal Soni

I WAS WRONG,

I BELIEVED!

Like a bad dream

it was all over

in a day or two.

Dreams which didn't take place

were already broken.

There was a change in voice,

not that usual, chirpy kind.

It was a moment of awe!

Making promises then,

just to break them now.

Oh, what a mess was created!

Trying to prove

as it was all okay.

They say that blood is thicker than water.

I didn't believe

but felt the pain, when it hurt me.

I WAS RIGHT,

I BELIEVED!

ೞ◈ಐ

First destroy, then you create.

They that know how to destroy

are those who don't know how to create.

Ones that do not know the first laugh,

the first cry for life.

Tears and dears, who taught this?

In the darkness, who held our hand

led us to an unknown way,

somewhere over a cut and connect.

Somethings are meant to be;

they happen in a way

like creating a Rubik's cube.

Colours, we see and assemble,

not understanding what roots

are

what leaves!

Ageing like fine wine

and maintaining a line

to calling it mine.

~❖~

It's pointless.

There are thousands of reasons

why it is.

An unshaped pencil is pointless.

Pointless to think over and wait.

It's an endless abyss.

One day we will all burn

with that the greed and vanity will go away.

Only gratitude will pay off.

The perfect form,

the perfect style, shape,

they list perfection, cast the net.

Last days will only be of hope,

the hope of comings.

Hope is a good thing,

maybe the best of things,

and no good thing ever dies.

Death comes to all,

don't be scared of it.

Reliving is the chance you get.

I am not scared of the darkness,

but, the deep ends.

Attachment is something not in my hands,

but detaching is.

I may overthink it often,

but I'm too deep into it.

Dead memories get brought back to mind,

but I jump to crazy imaginations.

The thought of those conversations spoil me,

but I tend to calm them.

A liar is my enemy,

but a veracious, is also not my friend.

Friends, lovers, a big terrible thing,

but, all that ends.

What if?

If we pretend it never happened.

The two words that spiral our lives,

beginning and end.

In a minute life takes a turn,

but, you don't turn away from life.

It's not the past what matters,

but the present.

For, I finding the correct way,

and, forgetting it all.

Life is like a book.

Some chapters are sad,

some are happy,

every word there, leaves with a meaning.

Indication to the next,

turn the page

to see the next chapter.

Cleaning after,

the perfect disaster!

Every word there, leaves with a meaning.

Indication to the next chapter,

cleaning after,

the perfect disaster!

Love is not meant for me.

It is that creepy feeling

which comes overtime

and develops a kind of passion,

that's not worth it.

Staying away from it, is also not an option.

Eventually, love attracts you

with its kind gestures

and leaves you with a mark

till it speaks with a whisper of art.

Don't be a part of it.

You never know where will it lead you

or you may lead it!

Those eyes

which once spoke

a thousand words,

sung stories

with sad endings,

made promises

in the dark.

Not realising it enough,

look ahead, what can you see?

I see a ray of sunshine,

a line of hope.

Let it be a thousand lies,

better than that unsaid truth.

☙◈❧

Time teaches you everything,

in a bliss of a minute.

Walking on the streets,

listening to some beats,

to the left of the sea,

and in the centre of a corner,

saw a girl standing

with a transparent umbrella

in this colourful, glassy world

full of deception.

Therefore, hidden appearances

are like the colour white,

which, one wants to turn in black,

not realising the existence of vibrants.

Serenity is no more a word,

just a saying.

Fickleness is present,

hustle and bustle.

It is a game of puzzle.

If all my wishes were to come true,

what would be left to do?

Worldly pleasures,

I have embraced all hardships

while staying unfazed

beyond what the eye can see.

The worthiness

so immersed in it,

forgot all sorrows

and focused along.

It's a sign of sadness

that triggers me,

a long way to go,

doing it all at once.

The greatest of all times,

showers words of wisdom,

knowingly surrenders itself to the wonders.

It's a blank screen

with colourful scenes.

Behind it, is hidden a huge mess,

unthinkable,

beyond all wildest dreams.

In the flurry of our beating hearts,

I asked for the moon,

they wanted peace.

There is never time enough;

our intimate dead, however, lie calm of face.

I have been seeing lonely people

in crowded rooms,

covered hearts

with drowned faces.

There may be distances

between the two,

but share a strong story.

Suffering from deep thoughts of curiosity,

she lost them

and never found them back.

Now, the existence is not felt,

but the pain is profound,

a never-ending misery,

and the hearts will keep heading

the mind wide open.

In a closed room

with such glimpses

that are invisible,

destiny that controls the world

never thus, it listens to us.

A different kind of pain

that is baffling

around the busy lives

of the people who are

now, adrift.

Being a part is not noticeable;

it's not your job to chase,

but to hold dear!

Even the ocean comes back to the shore.

What is love?

The leaves belong to the tree,

what are flowers?

The light gleams in the dark,

then wait for the daybreak?

It's not love,

merely a portrayal.

Love is that delight

that brings back the lost sight.

I wish, we could live in the pipe dream,

a complete delusion.

Live your story!

Passing by life,

those moments of love,

laughter, fall, cry.

That captivating smile,

charm of the red rose,

the sweet smell,

reminds me of the old days.

But now is a total change,

with calm eyes and

solitary,

ghosting scenes.

It all changes

with a bliss of one night,

where I stand before the waves,

moon shining gracefully,

exhaling the bad,

inhaling the good!

She moved the dirt away,

the stress from my shoulders.

Everyone moved away,

only she stayed,

and I was listening

to the delightful sound of rain.

Under the transparency

is a hidden thought

that no one knows about,

a broken truth.

The tables turned,

where you find the truth

you find your reflection,

which shows your inner soul,

which takes you to your happiness,

and there you see the lie for good,

which sets you free,

the harmless untruth!

�◈ఔ

NIGHT CHANGES

Impersonal the aim

Where there are played games,

And no one is the same,

But only one friend exclaims.

The true worth is explained,

That changes place like light.

They are all not named,

It disappears at night.

Life is not certain,

There are many ups and downs.

Times are uncertain,

Going out with the Browns.

Just a change of people and time,

Full of manipulations,

Some kind of drama every time;

At times, it gets to the point of frustration.

Having no regrets is all we want,

Only getting to know more.

It's like a beautiful story,

As soon as the night changes!

The universe is too big,

We are just a part of it.

The universe is unfolding as it should,

With something good.

People's mentality changed,

And so has their life.

Half are getting it rearranged;

Alas! They aren't dreams but the reality now.

I had a dream, a dream of dread,

With a lot of thoughts,

And memories all shred.

I thought that horror held lots.

We all live under the same sky,

With all the hustling, snoopy life.

When one day we have to say bye,

Some new people arrive.

Only the common stay,

For which explosion spoke.

And stiff on field and bay,

The dark blood of the folk.

When the time has come,

The sun is bright,

And the flowers are blooming.

We see the leaves dancing,

Waves.

Everything I have overcome has made me stronger.

The past is too deep.

The reflection of it is scary.

It happened because of a reason,

That is kept a secret.

I cried over it for a long time.

It hurt me immensely.

Now also it triggers my mind.

The only question is,

Why did it happen?

Problems are created by humans,

And even solved by them.

It is one which has just

Left a mark forever,

In my mind, my heart, and

My life.

The whole point of life

Is to change,

To grow,

To succeed,

To move on,

And never look back.

Count on the blessings,

Wish for the achievements.

Don't be remorseful about anything.

Today there was a piece of life,

That's something out of piece.

A missing touch or a quiet smile,

It's a cold and empty space,

Where it's a lonely group.

Despite the big number,

I only see a forgotten piece.

All the adulation from this world,

Nothing is in our hand.

It's Him who gives

And takes.

This life will pass,

And hurting them back

Will not heal the pain.

Like a horse,

Look straight

And find what is destined.

ॐ◈ॐ

There are sounds of death,

Sounds of happiness,

Sounds of cry.

Absence of sound,

Absence of reverberation,

Absence of life,

Leads to creation.

It progresses with productivity.

No one can stay mute.

How long can someone be silent?

ॐ◈ॐ

Everything is falling into pieces,

And those pieces are fitting

Into the exact places

Where they should be.

Perfection is not needed.

There is no place for darkness

Beneath the glittering stars

Is the hidden glory of the night.

It doesn't matter what you are doing,

In an unwavering way,

In a certain level of joy and wellbeing.

Unknowingly you stick somewhere,

Being clueless.

This world is round.

Your thoughts are unnoticed.

Your mind is revolving in circles.

You are not settled.

You are just moving,

Off and on, off and on.

A drive to a nearby place

Has led you to a different direction.

Happiness is the absence of grief,

And a clean soul is the presence of purity.

What does she deceive?

Yet again,

The sorrow and trouble in her heart

Is what makes it think.

And again,

Think of the past.

Never to repeat the sin.

Again,

Thy with a confession,

A true one!

This is for the one, someone who is special,

Who supported me in the dark,

When the moon was not shining.

She, who tied the knots,

And planted a kiss on my face,

In the lost grave.

She picked me up.

For a friend like her,

I would give up anything.

It's just the two of us!

☙ ◈ ❧

It all seems utterly meaningless

At the moment.

There is no one.

I'm stuck in a stage of

Yes or no,

Love and forgiveness,

Give and take.

Is it a game?

That is being played

With me?

Or with them?

Honesty speaks.

Truth will set you free,

But not until it is finished with you!

If you focus on your destiny,

you will definitely distance yourself

from making history.

It's not easy,

but not even impossible.

Live in the present,

spill out the tiny little things.

Your heart should not carry the load;

it's yours.

No problem can be solved

from the same level of consciousness

that formed it!

Life changes,

you lose love,

you lose friends,

but you don't lose yourself.

You gain a certain kind of power from within

when your soul senses it:

the divine timing of your life

is the way you look at it.

Happiness is content;

it is different for everyone,

as it should be!

When pain knocks on your door,

let it in

with ease in your heart,

calm eyes,

comforting it with happiness.

The love in you

is not meant to be tamed.

Let it out in the world

for whom it is meant.

Don't force things

which cannot happen.

If it is meant,

it may happen.

Friendships,

relationships,

boyfriend and girlfriend,

all end one day.

What doesn't end is you,

and you!

We are surrounded by so many people,

yet lonely.

These figures around

are meaningless,

a piece of dump

that is not meant for you.

It is said that,

before taking a step forward,

one trembles.

Before entering the sea,

the river trembles with fear.

She looks back at the past route

and thus, takes the new step forward.

 C3 ◈ 80

If love is meant to heal,

why does it hurt you the most?

If medicines are meant to cure,

why do they taste so bitter?

If that one person is meant for you,

why do they take time to be there?

It is said that,

the person who loves you...

It's all the twists and turns

of life

which got us to a certain stage.

There are happy people,

with sad eyes,

standing at the corner of every street,

all chaotic, waiting!

They may have strange laughs

to hide their soft cries.

The seasons that test your strength

are not the easy ones.

It's a mix of all,

sweet and sour, warm and cold,

under the open sky

where we all live

like the raindrops

and

like the sun shines.

There will be a difference

even through the darkness!

Is she hiding?

I saw a girl,

her hair was curled,

a smile on her face,

but does anyone know the real her?

The real feeling—

what all is she hiding?

She has curled up her thoughts

in her struggles and problems,

but manages to deal with them

on her own. No supports

and no reports.

What a girl!

But still, her friends wonder,

what all is she hiding?

Why the wait was necessary,

things take time—

it may be dark outside,

though, it's always brighter inside.

The truth, that the wait was necessary,

in the end, you shall get to know.

Trust the way it happens!

The end your heart wishes for,

when you find what's right for you,

all the good things will happen.

Truth wins all,

your work pays off.

With a positive attitude,

you get all,

and most importantly,

in the end, you shall know,

all loose ends find their place!

Some truths may not be heard the way they would—

but they linger, after long they've been said.

Little by little,

we all grow past

somethings that are better left unfound;

there are happier moments on the way

yet to discover!

Time and again, I wonder—

this—

is better than nothing at all.

It takes a minimum sacrifice

to be in a place you want.

That low point

is the key...

Everything is created twice,

once in your head and then in reality.

Eyes are loud,

actions are clear,

time takes us where we need to be.

No one thought of this major turn.

There are many bad stories;

choose what brings you peace.

It's not your fault,

for someone's inability to see

YOUR WORTH.

What matters to you,

might not matter to others.

At a point of time,

you will realise your loss;

it was beyond imagination.

Sometimes it takes absence to value presence,

sadness to feel happiness,

noise to appreciate silence.

Consider me a soul

you can always come talk to.

Even if it is the end of the world,

I will stand by you.

Any day, any time,

on good or bad terms,

I'm always there for you!

Sometimes life lessons can be tough,

comes with a little pain, hurt, laughter, cries.

But within all this lies the path to

growth and understanding.

If you don't experience pain,

you may not know the healing process

which is hidden within the pain.

Run from the pain

and you get further away from healing.

Have patience and reflect.

It may feel like your world is turning upside-down,

but it is only turning around for the better.

Guilt, pain, love or hate is not in your hand,

though, the control IS.

Control is something that should be focused on.

What if that control doesn't exist?

Like a river flows to the sea,

we must have the strength to walk

the paths that set us free.

Some are hidden paths

to new beginnings,

where you cannot find something you want,

but something you didn't think of coming.

Your worst battle is between yourself.

May you carry the seed of a

new start,

when the endings arrive.

You have to have a cold shoulder.

We all are lost at some point,

lost in thoughts, emotions,

greatness and weakness.

Lost in something we sought

is another thing!

Finding contentment in life

that's lost in our mind's shelves,

healing from that,

we never dwelt in.

This feeling is too controlling;

I just wish to escape!

At the end of the day,

it's all about yourself,

the way you think.

Your criticism is not taking you anywhere,

rather keeping you in a dark place

where it gets difficult to find the happy version.

But the irony here is,

your light grows stronger

when you are ready to face the darkness.

And that's when the light becomes our courage

to overcome tough days!

Being persevered

does not mean you are indifferent.

It certainly means,

being serene with being different.

Serenity and contentment

come with acceptance.

Why delve into what is beyond my control?

Transcend,

beyond what the eye can see!

What you think is the worst thing in your life

isn't the worst thing;

there is always something

that awaits you.

Feelings and emotions are temporary;

focus on what is permanent.

We evolve from being at our worst

to the best moment of our lives:

living through right now

to make it one of the

most powerful

parts of testimony!

I am an agonist,

not a protagonist.

Worrying is not in my hands,

but healing is.

Sometimes life teaches you those lessons

which only you can experience.

It lasted for a season

with its own reasons.

Confusion is better than,

ignorant conclusions.

When you fall in love with your

existence

rather than your

appearance,

it feels better.

Always be you,

listen to you,

live for you!

Ȣ◈ȵ

Connection and closeness

lead to sabotaging yourself

for something no one is responsible for

but you.

Attention is not love, nor is attachment;

it is that form of hurt

that leaves you disconnected

with reality.

ೠ◈ಔ

Peace is more precious

than perfection!

Not one of us can be at triumph

if our inner selves are not in harmony.

The strange stirring of silence occurs;

music heals.

Silence is a vast form of interiority;

it defines the space around you.

Your words seem black and white;

everything feels meaningless

behind the magic of the manifest

lies the unspoken trail

and the unspoken words—